It's All in Your Head!

by Angela Robinson

Welcome to the lab! To start building your Skull Model right away, turn to page 22!

It's All in Your Head!

Copyright becker&mayer!, 11010 Northup Way, Bellevue, Washington. Published 2004.

Published by SmartLab®, an imprint of becker&mayer!
All rights reserved. SmartLab® is a registered trademark of becker&mayer!, 11010 Northup Way, Bellevue, Washington.
Creative development by Jim Becker and Anna Johnson

No part of this book may be reproduced, stored in a retrieval system, or transmitted in any form or by any means, electronic, mechanical, photocopying, recording, or otherwise, without the prior permission of SmartLab®. Requests for such permissions should be addressed to SmartLab® Permissions, becker&mayer!, 11010 Northup Way, Bellevue, WA 98004.

If you have questions or comments about this product, send e-mail to info@smartlabtoys.com or visit www.smartlabtoys.com.

Edited by Betsy Henry Pringle
Written by Angela Robinson
Art direction and packaging design by Scott Westgard
Book design, interior art direction, and illustrations by Eddee Helms
Assembly illustrations by J. Max Steinmetz
Page 8 illustration by Stephan Kuhn
Page 16 illustration by Steve Kearsley © Exploratorium, www. exploratorium.edu
Page 20 illustration by Jennifer Fairman
Product photography by Keith Megay
SmartLab® character photography by Craig Harrold
Product development by Chris Tanner and Lillis Taylor
Production management by Katie Stephens
Project management by Beth Lenz

Every effort has been made to correctly attribute all the material reproduced in this book. We will be happy to correct any errors in future editions.

Printed, manufactured, and assembled in China.

It's All in Your Head! is part of the SmartLab® *Snap-together Skull Model* kit. Not to be sold separately.

10 9 8 7 6 5 4 3 2 1
0-9748486-8-9
03212

YOUR AMAZING BRAIN

When you dance and play, sing and paint, eat and sleep, run and walk, read and write, sniff and taste, see and touch, think and feel, you can tell your brain, Thank you! Without your brain, none of these things would be possible.

Your brain is what makes you a human being. It helps you learn about and understand the world around you. In this book, you'll learn about the many jobs your brain does for you. You'll explore the five senses through fun experiments. Along the way, you'll hear from Sammy Skull, and his pal Smart Lab.

Sammy Skull's my name and the brain's my game! Stick with me and Smart Lab and you'll be glad!

Your brain is a very special part of your body. Without your brain, you would not be **YOU**.

A BUNDLE OF BONES

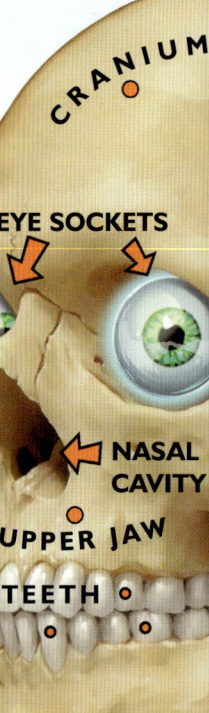

> Before you explore the brain, look at the wonderful bones that protect it!

> It's like this: Your body is a frame for your clothes to hang on, your skeleton is a frame for your organs to hang on, and your skin holds you in!

Your body is a bundle of bones—about 206 of them by the time you're fully grown. Bones are like a frame that gives your body its shape. They help you stand up and move around. They give your organs and muscles something to hold onto.

YOUR SKULL IS FULL

The part of your skeleton that holds your head is called your skull. It is made of 29 bones.

CRANIUM

SUTURES

Take a look at your assembled Sammy Skull. His skull is all the parts that are see-through. The top part of the skull is called the *cranium*. The jagged lines across the top of the cranium are *sutures*. These are where the soft cranial bones that babies are born with grew and fused together. All skulls have these funny-looking lines.

The front part of your skull has eye sockets, a nasal cavity, an upper jaw, a lower jaw, and teeth! If you haven't done this yet, press down on Sammy Skull's bony chin. In your body, muscles hold the lower jaw in place. For Sammy Skull, a rubber band does the job. Thanks to your moving jaw, you can chew and talk—but please don't do both at the same time!

YOUR SKULL IS FULL. OF WHAT?
YOUR BRAIN!

1. The liquid in more than four cans of soda can fit inside an empty adult skull.

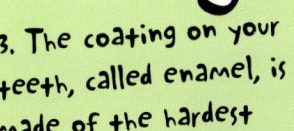

2. If you compare the strength of a steel bar and a bone of the same weight, the bone is MUCH stronger!

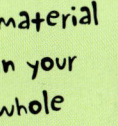

3. The coating on your teeth, called enamel, is made of the hardest material in your whole body.

5

EXPLORING THE

Now that you know about the skull, let's go inside it and explore the brain!

Lift up the top of Sammy's skull. See all the brown squiggles? That's the outside of his brain! If you could touch a real brain, it would feel like pudding. The squiggles (called folds and grooves) are there because your brain does a lot of growing from the time you are a baby to when you are a grown-up. This scrunched-up shape packs all this brain power into a little space. A lot of thinking happens in all those squiggles!

Pull out Sammy's brain. You'll see that there are two parts stuck together. Does that mean humans have two brains? No way!

BRAIN

Humans have one brain that is made of two parts, a right side and a left side. These two sides are called *hemispheres* (HEH-mes-feers). They are connected by a bunch of special nerve cells called *neurons* (nur-rons) that let both sides "talk" to each other.

THE BRAIN GETTING A MESSAGE

How does the brain send and receive messages? When you want to give someone a message, you can talk to them or write them a note. Your brain uses neurons to carry messages. Neurons are very tiny particles throughout your body. One neuron sends a message to the neuron next to it. That neuron sends the same message to the next neuron. This goes on and on until the message gets to its destination. Using neurons, the brain sends and receives messages very quickly.

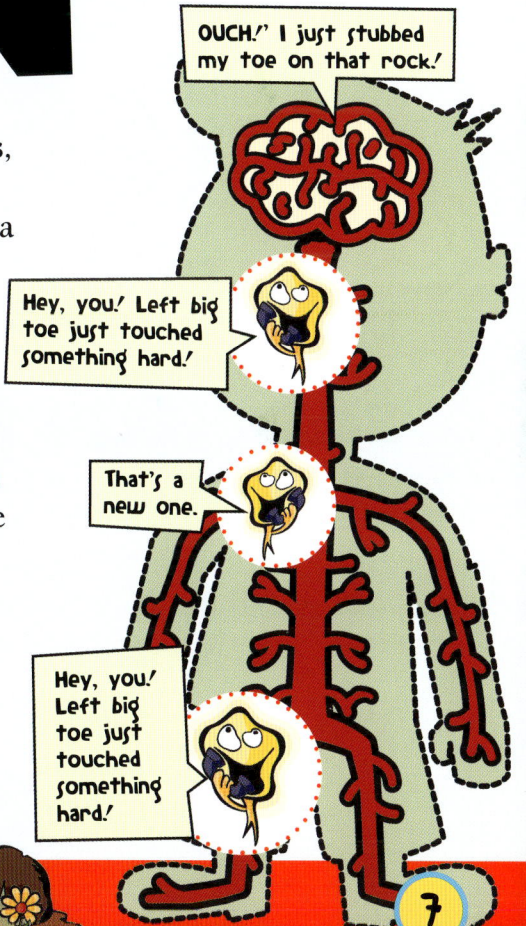

A DAY IN THE LIFE OF YOUR BRAIN

Your brain has a lot of jobs! Different parts of your brain help you do different things. Here are some things you do every day, and the parts of your brain that make them possible.

SAD? HAPPY? JUST RIGHT?

Feelings form in your brain, thanks to the *limbic* system. It has three parts: the *hippocampus* (hip-oh-CAMP-us), the *hypothalamus* (hi-po-THALL-uh-mus), and the *amygdala* (uh-MIG-duh-luh). Sadness, happiness, fear, pleasure, anger, hope, and all other feelings are controlled here.

WHAT'S YOUR NAME AGAIN?

So much to remember, every day! Names, numbers, events. The HIPPOCAMPUS helps you make memories.

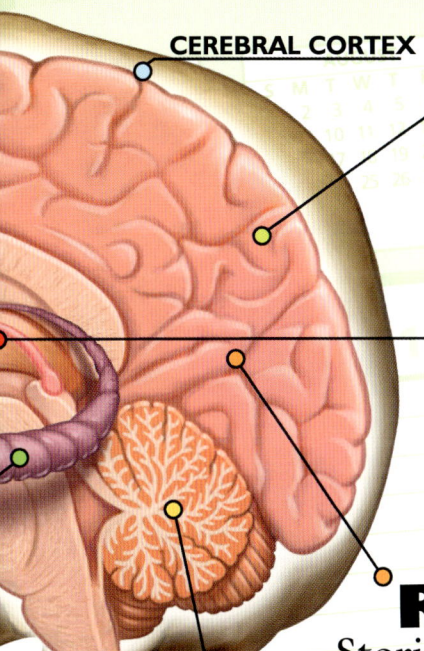

CEREBRAL CORTEX

BRAIN STEM

THINK, THINK, THINK!

The human brain is truly special. It can plan, use language, and put together information from the five senses. All this happens in the outer layer of the **CEREBRUM** (suh-REE-brum), called the *cerebral cortex*. This is the squiggly, bumpy part of the brain.

FEELING HUNGRY?

Your stomach is grumbling—almost time for lunch! The HYPOTHALAMUS tells you when it's time to eat and drink. When you get sleepy and need a rest, that's the hypothalamus giving you a message, too.

READ THAT BOOK!

Stories, poems, plays—so much to hear and read! WERNICKE'S (VER-nih-kuhs) area helps you understand language.

TIME FOR PLAYING!

Running, jumping, dancing, playing basketball! The CEREBELLUM (sare-uh-BELL-um) helps you be balanced and coordinated. The BRAIN STEM regulates your breathing, heart rate, and blood pressure.

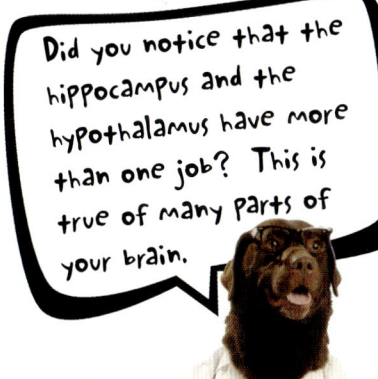

Did you notice that the hippocampus and the hypothalamus have more than one job? This is true of many parts of your brain.

SENSATIONAL SENSES

Now you're going to learn about the five senses: touch, sight, smell, taste, and hearing. As with other things you do, different parts of the brain control each sense.

TOUCH

Hot, cold, wet, dry, smooth, bumpy, soft, rough—skin is for touching!

When you touch something, your skin has different kinds of receptors that send messages to your brain. The message travels from your skin, through your spinal cord, and to your brain. The spinal cord is a long tube that goes all the way from the back of your neck to about halfway down your back. As you already learned, neurons pass the message along. Some areas of your body have more touch receptors than others. Your hands, for example, have many more touch receptors than your back.

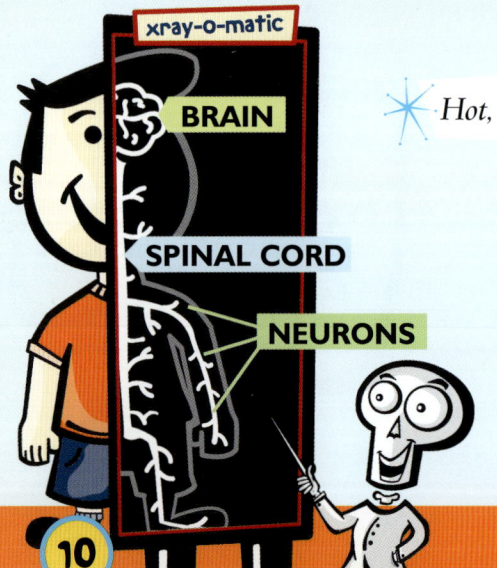

SAMMY SKULL'S
SENSORY SENSATIONS:
WHAT TO DO:

You can do this experiment on yourself if you don't have a helper handy! What you need: A paperclip

1. Open up the paperclip and bend it to make a U shape. Make sure that the tips of the U are even with each other.

2. Squeeze the U so that the tips are close together, but not touching.

3. Ask a helper to close his eyes and hold out his hand, palm down.

4. Touch the back of his hand lightly with both points of the paperclip. Does he feel one point or two?

5. Now, ask your helper (with his eyes still closed) to turn over his hand. Lightly touch the points of the paperclip to one of his fingertips. Does he feel one point or two?

6. Try touching your own leg, your lips, and other parts of your body.

7. Change the U shape so the two points are farther apart and try again. You might feel two points on your finger, but only one point on your calf. It all depends on how closely packed together the nerve cells are in different parts of your skin.

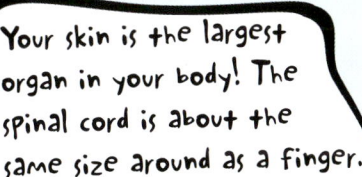

Your skin is the largest organ in your body! The spinal cord is about the same size around as a finger.

SIGHT

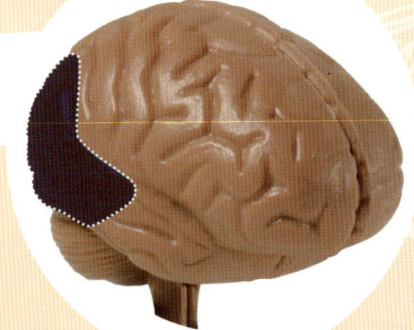

✦ *Colors, shapes, faces, motion—eyes are for seeing!*

By now, you have probably noticed Sammy Skull's glow-in-the-dark eyes. Let Sammy sit in bright light for a few minutes, and then take him to a dark place (a closet works great). See his bright green eyes? Pretty creepy!

Like Sammy's eyes, your eyes are ball shaped. They sit in bony sockets that help protect the parts of the eyes that you can't see.

Sammy Says, "I love it when it's bright. I get spooky when it's night!"

HUMANS VIEW!

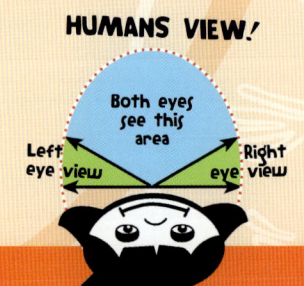

Both eyes see this area. Left eye view. Right eye view.

DOGS VIEW!

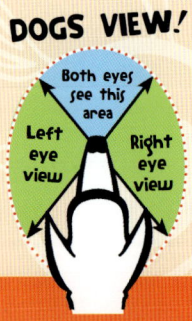

Both eyes see this area. Left eye view. Right eye view.

12

LIGHT

IMAGE

The first ingredient you need for seeing is light. Light bounces off of objects and comes into your eyes through your *pupils*. Light then passes through a lens, and the image is shined onto the back of your eyeball, the *retina*. The lens bends the light, making the image appear upside down on your retina!

Luckily, your brain sorts this all out. The optic nerves send messages about what you see to your brain. The world looks wonderfully right side up!

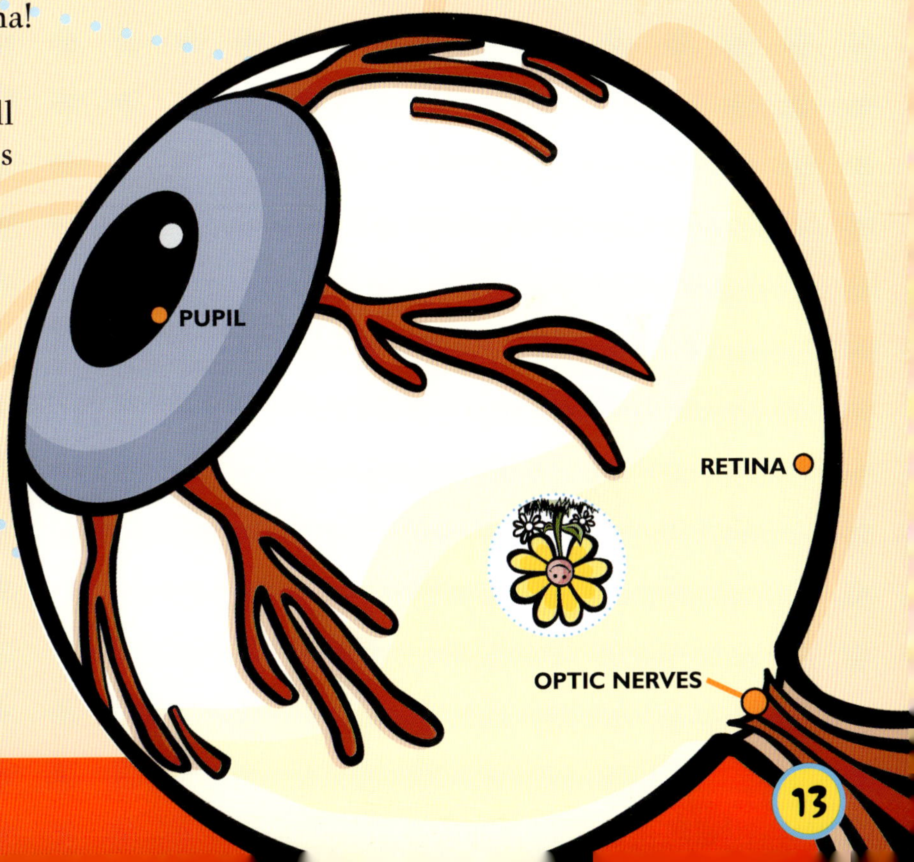

Dogs don't see as well as humans. I guess that's why I've got these glasses!

PUPIL

RETINA

OPTIC NERVES

13

SAMMY SKULL'S SENSORY SENSATIONS: OPTICAL

WHICH DO YOU SEE— A VASE OR TWO FACES?

WHAT'S HAPPENING?

You will notice that it is difficult to see both the faces and the vase at the same time.

Your eyes send both images to your brain, but your brain has to choose which one you see.

ILLUSIONS

SEE-THROUGH HAND

Roll up a piece of paper and look through it with one eye. Keep both eyes open and stare into the distance. Bring your other hand (or another object) a few inches in front of the eye that is not looking through the tube.

Keep looking with both eyes into the distance. You'll see a hole in your hand! (If you stop looking into the distance and instead look at your hand, the hole magically disappears!)

WHAT'S HAPPENING?

Your eyes are set apart, so each eye sees a slightly different image. When you focus on a distant spot, nearby objects are out of focus. This can cause the two images to overlap.

SMELL

Dogs have a much better sense of smell than humans. This is because dogs have many more scent receptors than humans do—200 million of them, compared to 5 million in humans. Have you noticed that you can't smell well when you have a cold? That's because your scent receptors are blocked.

✴ *Flowers, cake, shampoo, dirt—noses are for smelling!*

Behind the top of your nose, deep inside where you can't see, are two important things: hair and snot. Yuck! But without these tiny hairs (cilia), and snot (mucus), you wouldn't be able to smell!

Imagine that you are smelling cookies baking in the oven. The cookies are giving off little bits of scent that are too small for you to see. These bits travel from the oven up the cilia inside your nose, where they get mixed with mucus. The mucus carries the particles to your smell receptors. The olfactory bulb in your brain recognizes the scent and you think, Yum! Chocolate chip cookies!

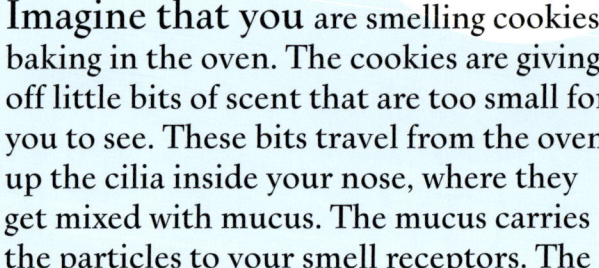

SAMMY SKULL'S SENSORY SENSATIONS:
MATCH THAT SMELL

WHAT YOU NEED:
- At least six plastic containers with lids (not see-through) Yogurt containers would be good.
- A fork for punching holes
- Smelly things (roses, orange peel, garlic, coffee grounds, dirt, etc.)

WHAT TO DO:

1. Place the smelly things into containers. Make two containers of each item. Have an adult help you poke holes in the tops of the containers so you can smell what's inside them.

2. Mix the containers up and see if you can match containers that have the same item.

3. What smells are easier to recognize? Which ones are more difficult?

TASTE

Sweet, salty, sugary, tangy—tongues are for tasting!

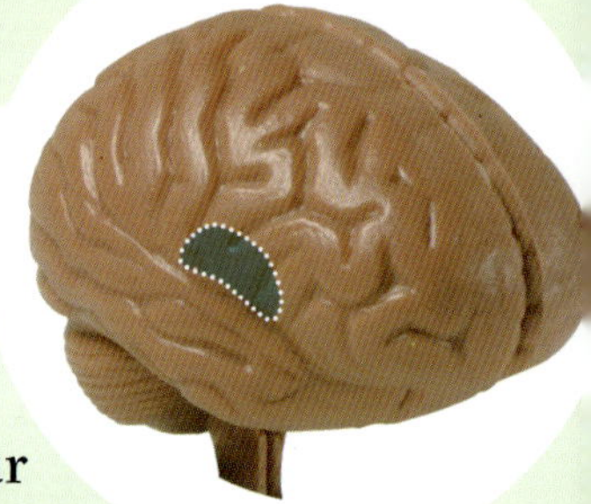

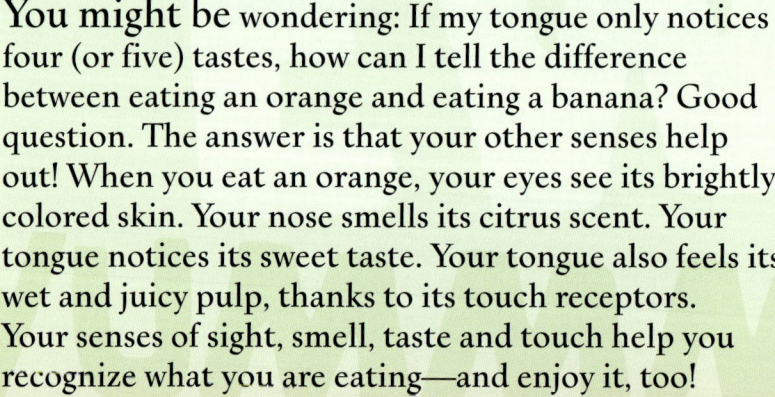

Look in a mirror and stick out your tongue. Do you see all those little bumps? Many of the bumps have taste buds inside them. These taste buds send messages to your brain. You may be surprised to learn that your tongue only notices four tastes: sour, sweet, salty, and bitter. Some scientists also think there is a fifth taste called *umami* (oo-mom-ee), but this taste is hard to describe. Perhaps this fifth taste is yumminess.

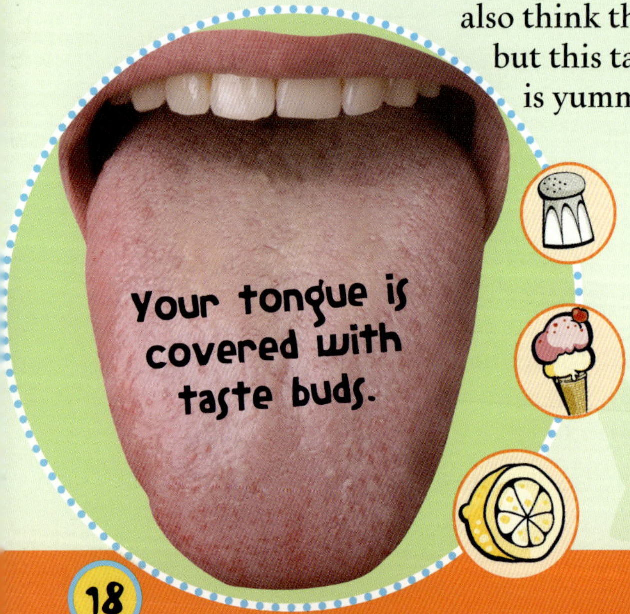

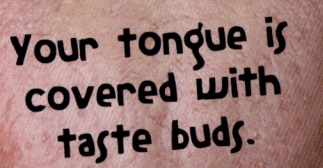

Your tongue is covered with taste buds.

You might be wondering: If my tongue only notices four (or five) tastes, how can I tell the difference between eating an orange and eating a banana? Good question. The answer is that your other senses help out! When you eat an orange, your eyes see its brightly colored skin. Your nose smells its citrus scent. Your tongue notices its sweet taste. Your tongue also feels its wet and juicy pulp, thanks to its touch receptors. Your senses of sight, smell, taste and touch help you recognize what you are eating—and enjoy it, too!

SAMMY SKULL'S SENSORY SENSATIONS:
CAN YOU TASTE WITHOUT SMELL?

Have an adult help you cut and peel the apple and potato.

WHAT YOU NEED:
- Apple slices (with the skin peeled)
- Potato slices (also with the skin peeled)
- A blindfold
- A nose plug (or your fingers!)

You have about 10,000 taste buds to help you enjoy what you eat. Your tongue also helps you to swallow and to speak.

WHAT TO DO:

1. **Ask a friend** or adult if they'd like to do a taste-testing experiment. Cover your partner's eyes with the blindfold and have her plug her nose. Place either an apple slice or a potato slice on her tongue. See if she can guess which is which, without chewing! (Not chewing is important because the texture of the food gives clues about it.)

2. **Have your partner** unplug her nose, and try the experiment again. See if she can tell the difference between the apple and the potato when she can smell it and taste it. Now, you try!

HEARING

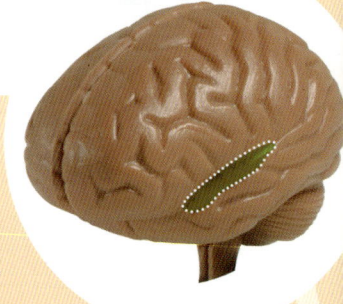

Whispers, shouts, laughter, singing—ears are for hearing!

Ears come in all shapes and sizes. They never stop growing. Some ears have hearing aids. Hearing aids help people who have lost some of their ability to hear. Some ears have earrings! ALL ears have wax. Why is that? Wax keeps your ears healthy—it traps dirt and other things that get into your ears, and it sends them back out!

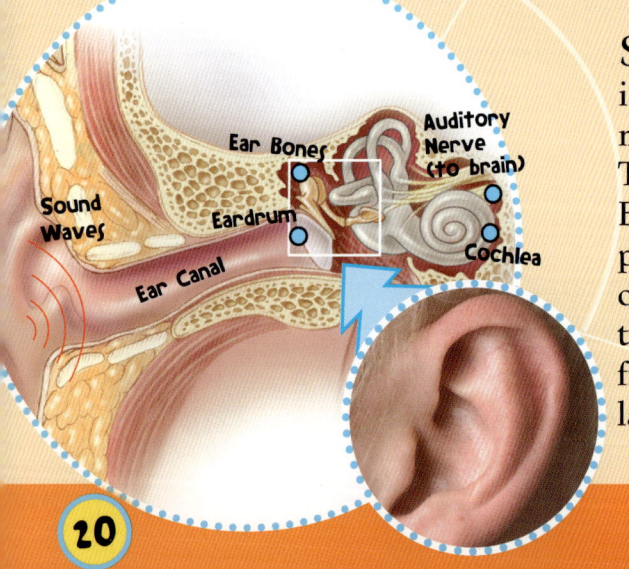

Sounds are vibrations in the air. They travel into your ears through the *ear canal*. The vibrations make a thin flap of skin, called the *eardrum*, vibrate. Three tiny bones near the eardrum vibrate, too. Eventually, these vibrations reach tiny hairs in a place called the *cochlea* (KO-cle-uh). At the bottom of each hair is a nerve cell. These nerve cells send the messages to the brain. Now you can hear your friend's secret, your playmate's shouts, your father's laughter, and your grandmother's singing.

SAMMY SKULL'S SENSORY SENSATIONS: WHERE'S THAT SOUND?

WHAT YOU NEED:
- Blindfold
- Object such as a small bell or a set of keys

WHAT TO DO:
Ask a friend if you can blindfold him. Have him cover one ear with his hand. Choose an object for making sounds. Make the sound near your friend's covered ear. Now, slowly move away, farther and farther from his ear. Keep making the sound. When does your friend stop hearing the sound? Try this again with both ears uncovered. Is it easier for your friend to hear? Now, switch places and try it yourself!

ASSEMBLY INSTRUCTIONS

Compare the pieces that came with your kit to the pieces in this labeled illustration. Now, follow these steps to assemble your skull model.

1) POP IN THE UPPER TEETH
a. The upper teeth are marked with a "U."
b. Insert the upper teeth pegs into the holes in the upper jaw.

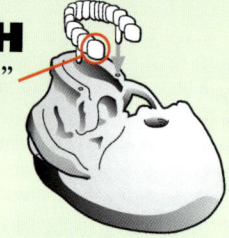

2) MOUNT THE UPPER JAW
a. Find the lower jaw and hold it upside down.
b. Fit the ball joints on the lower jaw into the sockets on the base of the skull.
c. The rubber band that is attached to the lower jaw should hang into the zygomatic arch.
d. Pull the rubber band through the zygomatic arch and loop it over the hook on the skull.
e. Repeat the process on the other side of the skull using the other rubber band.

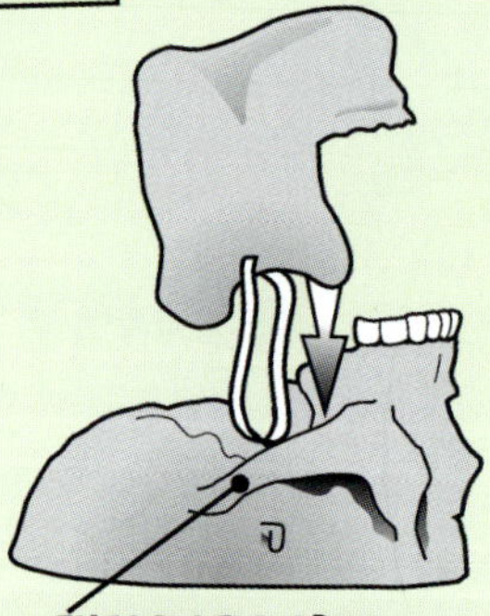

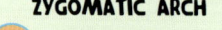
ZYGOMATIC ARCH

3) INSERT THE LOWER TEETH
a. Turn the skull over.
b. Holding the skull in your hand, gently open the mouth and insert the lower teeth pegs into the holes in the lower jaw. (Be careful! Don't let your fingers get caught between the teeth.)

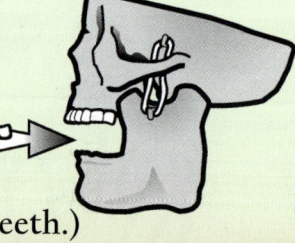

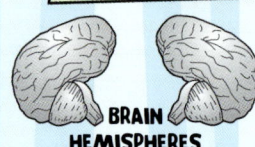
BRAIN HEMISPHERES

EYEBALLS
UPPER TEETH
SQUARE PEGS
LOWER TEETH
SHAFT
ROUND PEGS

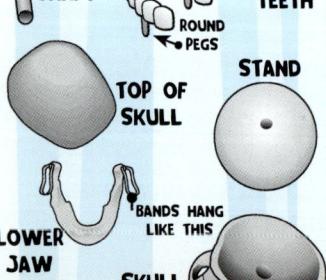
TOP OF SKULL
STAND
LOWER JAW
BANDS HANG LIKE THIS
SKULL

22

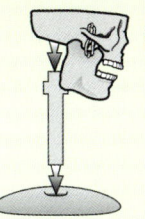

④ MOUNT THE SKULL STAND

  a. One end of the shaft has a collar or ring on it.
  b. Insert the end with the collar into the hole in the base of the skull.
  c. Insert the other end of the shaft into the hole in the stand.

⑤ POP IN THE EYES

  a. Notice that the eyeballs have long stems.
  b. Push the stem of one eyeball into one of the sockets. Press gently until the end fits into the hole at the back of the socket. (The eyes are the same, so either eyeball can be inserted into either socket.)
  c. Do the same with the other eye.

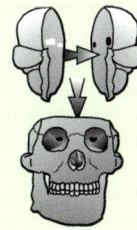

⑥ ASSEMBLE THE BRAIN

  a. Insert the pegs on one hemisphere of the brain into the holes on the other.
  b. The brainstem—that little "tail" pointing down—fits through the hole in the base of the skull. Place the brain into the lower skull.

⑦ CLOSE THE SKULL

  a. The top of the skull has two pegs. One peg is marked with a "B." ("B" is for back.)
  b. Fit the peg marked "B" into the hole on the back of the lower skull. The other peg fits into the hole on the front of the skull.

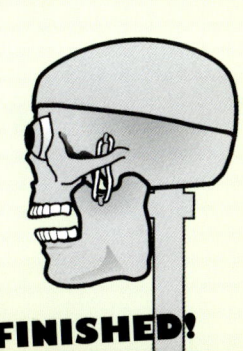

FINISHED!

New discoveries about the brain are being made all the time by people (and some very smart dogs) called *neuroscientists* (ner-oh-sigh-un-tists). You can be a neuroscientist, too! Just pay attention to all the ways your brain helps you enjoy life.

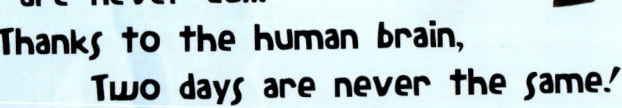

When you've got a full skull,
Things are never dull.
Thanks to the human brain,
Two days are never the same!

Do you like to think?
Do you like to run?
Do you like to play games in the bright sun

Then it's plain as plain,
Take good care of your brain!

Try to eat right,
And wear a helmet on your bike!
Get plenty of rest,
This helps your brain do its best!

THANKS FOR GETTING BRAINY WITH SMARTLAB!